MARGRET

CW00394800

BEADS AND BEADWORK OF WEST AND CENTRAL AFRICA

SHIRE ETHNOGRAPHY

Cover photograph
The woman in the centre holds a bowl with a bird on the cover; the two attendants hold a staff with a bird on top and a flute. The bowl is for containing kolanuts, which were an important item of tribute, and which might be presented to important guests. This model was collected before 1912. Yoruba, south-western Nigeria. Height 25.5 cm (10.1 inches).
(Museum of Mankind, London.)

British Library Cataloguing in Publication Data:
Carey, Margret.
Beads and Beadwork of West and Central Africa.
— (Shire ethnography).
1. Africa. Central Africa. West Africa.
Central and West Africa. Beadwork.
I. Title.
746. 5096.
ISBN 0-7478-0100-2.

For my very good friends William Fagg and the late Bryan Cranstone, who got me involved with ethnography and beads.

Published by
SHIRE PUBLICATIONS LTD
Cromwell House, Church Street, Princes Risborough,
Buckinghamshire HP17 9AJ, UK.

ISBN 0 7478 0100 2

First published 1991.

Printed in Great Britain by
C. I. Thomas and Sons (Haverfordwest) Ltd,
Press Buildings, Merlins Bridge, Haverfordwest, Dyfed.

Contents

Acknowledgements

I am grateful to Dr John Mack for reading the typescript and for his advice, and to Bernard Brandham for his work in processing my photographs; also to Professor Allen Roberts, Professor Frank Willett and Mrs Marilee Wood for helping me with the use of their photographs; and to the following museums and their staff for permission to publish many of the illustrations and for their help generally: Museum of Mankind, London; Pitt Rivers Museum, Oxford; National Museums of Scotland, Edinburgh; Powell-Cotton Museum, Birchington; Musée Royal de l'Afrique Centrale, Tervuren, Belgium; University of Iowa Museum of Art, Iowa City, USA. As ever, I am grateful to my husband for his support.

The cover picture and the photographic illustrations are by the author except where otherwise credited in the captions. The map on page 7 is by D. R. Darton.

4

List of illustrations

1
Introduction

Beads and Beadwork of East and South Africa gave a background to the subject of beadwork from that area and provided some guidelines to help with identification. This book does the same for western and central Africa, but it takes a somewhat different form. The writings of early travellers combine with archaeology to give us more historical background to the role of beads and beadwork in trade and society. We know that there were many stable agricultural communities which formed a setting for the prestige beadwork found in Ghana, Nigeria, Cameroon and Zaire. Beads were the monopoly of kings and chiefs who controlled them through trade or tribute from the outside world. Since the ownership of beaded masks was in the hands of priests and important people, beaded royal and religious regalia and beaded masks were restricted to an elite minority. At the same time, beadwork as ornament or clothing was worn by ordinary people. Thus there may be two different types of beadwork found in the same area.

Knowledge of beads and beadwork in western and central Africa can be patchy; if none is mentioned from a particular area, it may mean simply that none has been collected or studied, since, with a few exceptions, the subject has not been taken seriously until recently. Early collectors tended to be more interested in weapons and 'curios' than beads and beadwork, so that often all we have is a passing mention or, with luck, a tantalising photograph or watercolour which may provide the only surviving evidence for the beadwork of a particular area.

Unlike much southern African beadwork, which is made with strong sinew thread, that of western and central Africa is usually strung on cotton, vegetable fibre or raphia thread, which is liable to snap or disintegrate; as a result, beadwork over a hundred years old may not have survived.

Beads were a form of currency from the earliest days of European trade and exploration; market preferences had to be carefully studied and bead manufacturers and dealers used sample cards to display their wares (figure 1). During the colonial period some administrations used beads as a means of economic control; forced labour might be paid for only in beads which could be exchanged at government-run stores, which bought them in a limited range of colours and types.

For the purpose of this study, West and Central Africa is an area extending from Senegal in the west to Zaire and Lake Tanganyika in the east, and from the Sahara in the north to southern Angola and Zaire. The period covered, unless otherwise qualified, is that of the 'ethnographical present', which covers the time from the nineteenth-century exploration period onwards to about the start of the Second World War. Beads sometimes have a symbolic value, while beadwork gives insights into tribal culture and the status of its members. Beads can possibly indicate when trade contacts began and confirm site dating; archaeology is providing potentially useful cross-references from beads in carbon-dated American Indian or Caribbean sites in the Americas. Beads can even outline vanished clothing and ornaments.

Map of West and Central Africa showing countries, towns and tribes mentioned in the text. Towns and sites are denoted by an asterisk in the following key; the other names are tribes: 1, Asante; 2, Bachama; 3, Bamileke; 4, Bamoun; 5, Bassari; 6, Benin*; 7, Bida*; 8, Bobo-Fing; 9, Dowayo; 10, Fang; 11, Fernando Po*; 12, Fulani; 13, Ibibio; 14, Ibo; 15, Ife*; 16, Igbo-Ukwu*; 17, Ilorin*; 18, Kalabari; 19, Kirdi; 20, Krobo; 21, Kuba; 22, Jenne-Jeno*; 23, Jokwe; 24, Kwanyama; 25, Luba; 26, Lunda; 27, M'Pongwe; 28, Ngbaka; 29, Nok*; 30, Ovambo; 31, Sara Madjingai; 32, Sherbro; 33, Tabwa; 34, Timbuktu*; 35, Tiv; 36, Tuareg; 37, Walata*; 38, Yaka; 39, Yoruba.

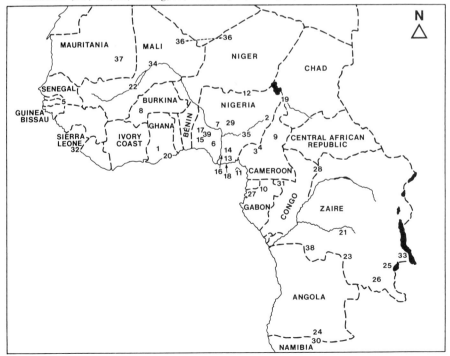

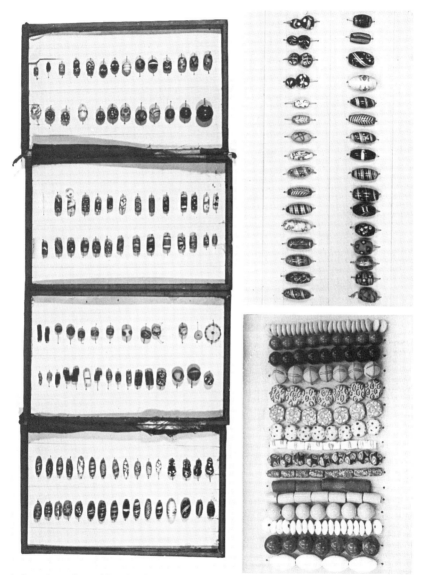

1. Sample cards used in selecting beads for trade with Africa. (Left) Folder of trade beads used by the explorer Henry Morton Stanley, probably used 1870-89. (Right above) Detail of one card from the Stanley folder. (Copyright: Musée Royal de l'Afrique Centrale, Tervuren, Belgium.) (Right below) 'Beads such as are used by traders in West Africa, & given in exchange for Palm Oil & other African produce.' Datable to 1857-69. (Museum of Mankind, London.)

2
Bead types

The word 'bead' is defined in the *Oxford English Dictionary* as a 'small perforated body, spherical or otherwise, of glass, amber, metal, wood, etc, used as an ornament, either strung in a series to form a necklace, bracelet, etc or sewn upon various fabrics'.

Nearly all beads have to be shaped, whether made of shell, wood, clay, stone, metal or glass. In Africa, archaeology shows that tin and stone beads were made towards the end of the first millennium BC.

The beads found in West and Central Africa are made of both natural and man-made materials. As in East and South Africa, beads made of seeds, wood and clay were used and may have been represented on the late first-millennium BC terracottas from Nok, Nigeria. Such beads would not survive in a normal archaeological context. Those of shell, stone, metal, coral and glass do, and the study of these shows that there was a great deal of early trade and culture contact.

Some beads are made from shells that were simply pierced, such as cowries, olivellas and colourful snail-shells. Disc beads are made from the shells of ostrich eggs, clams or large snails. The shells are broken into rough blanks, pierced, strung together and then ground and polished on a stone to finish them. Coconut and other seed-cases and, recently, plastic are used to make disc beads in the same way.

Stone beads are troublesome to make when using traditional tools. Such beads may be recognised by the biconical and often crooked perforation from both ends. Stones used were agate, red jasper, bauxite, serpentine and soapstone. The making of stone beads in Ilorin and other places is described below. Agate and carnelian beads were also imported from Cambay in western India from at least the first century AD; from 1830 to 1840 Idar-Oberstein in Germany produced millions of beads in similar style, using first local and then Brazilian agate. The beads include long faceted beads, are more highly finished than the Indian ones, and the hole is slightly enlarged at both ends to avert wear on the string.

Glass beads were imported from outside Africa, whether from Europe or India. Glass copies of carnelian and banded agate beads, coral, copal amber, conus shells, lions' teeth and claws were made in Jablonec (Gablonz) in Czechoslovakia.

To date, the earliest glass beads found in West Africa are those from Igbo-Ukwu, in southern Nigeria; they are carbon-dated to AD 700-1020. It is uncertain where these beads come from; there are two chemical groups, one of which seems to be of European origin; the other may be from the Near East or India. Venice started making glass during the fifth century, but it is not yet certain when glass beads were first made there — perhaps in the eleventh century. There were glass-bead workshops in the eastern Mediterranean, which could have supplied Igbo-Ukwu.

The three basic methods of making glass beads are discussed in chronological order of appearance and complexity. To make *wound* beads, the heated, plastic glass is wound round a wire mandrel and is marvered (rolled or pressed) into shape. Swirl marks and tiny air bubbles at right angles to the hole identify these beads. Then come *drawn* beads, where an air bubble is trapped inside a glass gather, which is then rapidly drawn out into a long tube, which, after cooling in a special rack, is chopped into short lengths. Such beads may be finished off by heat-tumbling to remove the sharp cut edges. This method greatly speeded up beadmaking; most beads found in Africa, notably the small round beads often called 'seed' or 'pound' beads, belong to this group. Drawn beads often show air bubbles or stripes running parallel to the hole. Recent research suggests that drawn-glass beads were made in India from the early centuries AD. *Moulded* (or 'tile') beads appeared in the nineteenth century; the Prosser process was patented in 1840, and most of these beads come from Czechoslovakia. They can be recognised by the seams where the moulds joined. Plastic beads are a twentieth-century innovation. 'Lamp' beads (figure 14) are an elaboration of wound beads where the bead is decorated on the surface with molten glass in relief or contrast colour pattern; 'eye' beads, found in West, Central and East Africa, are well known; others occur in Ghana and Nigeria. The elaborate chevron or star-rosetta beads, usually layered in blue, red and white (figure 25), millefiori or mosaic beads (figure 14) and extra large beads all signify rank.

Even though glass beads entered Africa in almost unbelievable quantity, Africans themselves made their own. Early travellers described how beads would be cut into smaller sizes or ground to a preferred shape. In Ife, Nigeria, analysis of the glass in crucible fragments points to the melting down of imported glass; the droplets of melted glass were perforated as if of stone. In more recent times, two basic types of African-made glass beads occur, apart from imported glass fragments pierced, ground and polished into beads. The processes are described below.

Coral comes from the Mediterranean, as the seas off western Africa do not produce it. Before 1472, when the Portuguese first arrived in western Africa, it may have come across the Sahara. Coral beads are especially important in Benin, Nigeria, where they form the major element in the ceremonial costume of the Oba (king). Among the Ibo and other peoples in southern Nigeria, numerous and massive coral beads are important status symbols. Coral beads became a major import although 'coral' in early accounts often means simply 'bead' (derived from the Dutch *kralen*).

Amber is used for prestige beads, especially in the Sahel. This amber seems to have come from the Baltic; today many amber beads are copal (usually from the Zanzibar coastal region and traded overland). Glass imitations of amber are easily recognised by the weight and coldness. Plastic amber may be sold in rods and cut and polished to shape; it is harder to distinguish from copal or true amber without expert testing.

Beadmaking in West Africa

In western Africa, before the mass import of beads from Europe, people made their own. Seeds, shell, bone, wood, clay, metal, stone and even glass were used. Some of these locally made beads rate special description.

In the Timbuktu area of Mali, beads are made of fine blond straw elaborately twisted and plaited on to a beeswax core. They appear to imitate gold filigree work such as that of Senegal and are said to have been invented by a woman in 1938. Beads of various shapes are strung in necklaces; straw is also used to make

2. Necklace with three beads of plaited straw, from Timbuktu, Mali. (National Museums of Scotland, Edinburgh.)

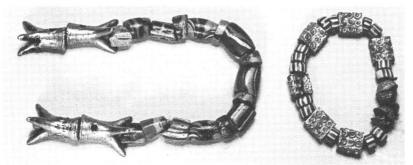

3. Two strings of Venetian trade beads with hollow-cast gold beads. Those on the left are stylised human molars. Collected in Asante, Ghana, before 1890. (Museum of Mankind, London.)

earrings, pendants and bracelets. Owing to its perishable nature and fragility, such adornment is reserved for special occasions (figure 2).

Metal filigree work, which the straw beads seem to have imitated, is made in Senegal, the Ivory Coast and Ghana, using the lost-wax process. In this, beeswax is rolled into fine strands, which are assembled into the desired form and encased in a mould. After the wax has been burnt out, the molten metal, usually gold, silver or brass, is poured in. After cooling, the casting jets (remains of the metal pouring) and irregularities are trimmed off and the bead is ready. Gold and silver beads, because of the metal value, are usually hollow (figure 3), whether filigree or not.

Stone beads are found especially in Ghana and Nigeria; Ilorin, a town in northern Yorubaland, is an important source. Tradition says that the craft was brought there by refugee or slave emigrants from Old Oyo, the ancient Yoruba capital, in about the 1830s. Red jasper, banded agate or chalcedony were imported by Hausa traders who brought it from Niger to Ilorin for processing. These beads were called *lantana* and were widely traded over much of Nigeria; buyers might travel 350 km (225 miles) to get them. Beadmaking was reserved to specialist Yoruba families; the work was done mostly by men, but women shared in the grinding and polishing. The industry seems to have died out now, perhaps as a result of overproduction in the period after the First World War. Efforts to revive the industry failed, partly because of official discouragement in the 1940s and 1950s, partly because the process was time-consuming and relatively ill paid. In the mid 1930s one bead might fetch between 2 old pence and 2 shillings sterling, depending on size and quality. A stone piece was roughly shaped, then held between the maker's toes while, using a succession of up to sixty small fine steel nail-shaped drills with palm-oil lubricant and a tiny hammer, he pecked out the perforation from both ends till the holes met. It seems to have taken over three hours to drill a 2.5 cm (1 inch) hole, and a day's output might be only two or three beads, since, after shaping and piercing, each bead had to be ground and polished.

Lantana beads were mostly long and cylindrical, barrel-shaped or biconical; they were bought by chiefs or rich people as prestige jewellery and are still treasured despite competition from the cheaper stone and glass imitations and other beads made in Europe. The beadmakers also made pendants and peg-like stone ear plugs and lip plugs, which are no longer fashionable but are shown on some Yoruba wood-carvings.

In Ghana bauxite (aluminium ore), a mottled pinkish-red stone of varying hardness, was mined in the south, in the Birim valley.

4. Glass-workers at work in Bida, northern Nigeria. (From an oil painting by Carl Arriens, 1911.)

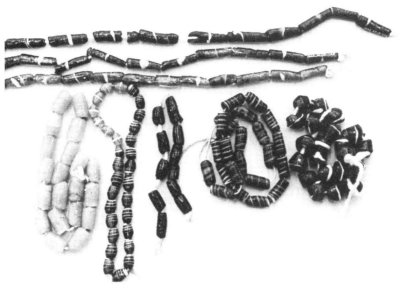

5. A selection of glass beads from Bida, northern Nigeria. (Museum of Mankind, London.)

Bead blanks, usually about 1 cm (⅜ inch) thick, were cut to shape with an iron knife on a wooden anvil and perforated with a bow-drill. The pierced beads were threaded on to a raphia palm thread or, if available, a bicycle-wheel spoke before grinding down to shape on a grooved stone. Such beads were strung on raphia and worn for ornament by women and children; up to nine girdle strings of the largest size, about 2 cm (¾ inch), was the accepted minimum in the early 1940s, when a single girdle string might cost 1s 6d sterling. Tradition suggests that this craft was flourishing one hundred years before that; the beads were traded all over Ghana, to Lagos in Nigeria, and especially to the Ivory Coast. Harder stone such as serpentine was also made into beads; these had a high prestige value.

Bida, a town in Nupe country in northern Nigeria, was another home of stone beadmaking, although it is better known for its distinctive barrel-shaped beads and bangles made of recycled glass. The process has changed little since it was described by Leo Frobenius in 1911, and there are many accounts of Bida and its glass-workers, who claim that they came from Egypt in about the first half of the eighteenth century.

The glass-workers work in groups of five (figure 4) around a small wood-burning furnace set in the floor of a hut with

6. String of Krobo beads made in southern Ghana. Figure 1 (right below), fourth row from the top, shows Venetian copies of this sort of bead. (Museum of Mankind, London.)

triangular openings cut in the walls to provide some light and ventilation. The furnace is brought to a good heat with bellows, and a gather of molten glass made from salvaged beer bottles and other glass scraps is prepared; colour may be added in the form of European glass beads. Bead colours include blackish brown, green, yellow, clear brown and blue; the distinctive white spiral trail (figure 5) comes from white beads melted down and added while the bead is still hot. The bead-worker has a long spit which he dips into muddy water to keep the glass from sticking; he then picks up a little melted glass, which he turns rapidly while patting the bead into shape with a spatula; the white glass is picked up with tongs, held in the flame and wound on to the twirling bead, which is then shaken off and left to cool. The glass-workers can make fifteen to twenty beads in a minute; they are organised into a guild which manages the workshops, pays the men's wages on a piecework basis and controls the output. The beads are sold, usually by middlemen, over most of Nigeria and as far afield as Senegal and Mali. Bida glass-workers also made their own glass (*bikini*) out of raw materials; this is densely black and is mixed with recycled glass and used for making bangles.

The 'powder-glass' process of beadmaking is widely found in Africa; the earliest known are the cylindrical 'garden-roller' beads of Zimbabwe, south-eastern Africa. They seem to have been made of powdered beads of the same chemical composition as those found in some archaeological sites and are perhaps twelfth-century AD. Thomas Bowdich wrote in 1819 of 'boiled beads' which were clearly of powder-glass; the process may have been in use among the Asante of Ghana for three centuries.

The Krobo and other peoples of southern Ghana make beads by the powder-glass process, involving the use of pulverised European glass bottles and beads. Such beads are usually called 'Krobo' (figure 6), *adjagba* or *bodom* beads. Clay moulds (figure 7) are prepared and each cavity is filled with powdered glass; a small green leaf-stem in the centre forms the perforation. Since it is green, it does not char until the glass powder fuses. The mould is fired in a small furnace, not hot enough to melt the glass, but enough to cause partial fusion of the particles. The surface, even after grinding to shape and light polishing, tends to be matt, with traces of layering at right angles to the perforation. Sometimes the glass powder is carefully layered to form bands of colour (figure 7); by poking a groove down the side, a trail-like stripe of contrast colour is made by trickling glass powder into the hole. Surplus glass powder is carefully brushed away with a feather. Yellow beads with contrast in green and black are popular and were imitated by Venetian beadmakers (figures 1 and 6). Blue 'Milk of Magnesia' bottles make blue beads; Pond's cold-cream pots make opaque white beads; ingots of coloured Venetian glass, if and when available, might have been used for colouring.

Freeman, writing in 1898, described glassworking in Bontuku

7. Bead-making outfit as used in Dunkwa, southern Ghana, in the 1930s. On the left, cullet scraps; on the right, beads made in a mould of this type. (Museum of Mankind, London.)

in northern Ghana, where armlets were made from softened glass cullet and coloured glass seed beads to create a marbled effect. Glass beads could have been made in Bontuku but were not recorded. In Mali powder-glass beads imitating gneiss occur.

An extraordinary group of powder-glass beads comes from Kiffa and Walata (Oualata) in Mauritania, which have been described by Jean Gabus and others. The beads resemble millefiori but are made of white glass powder mixed to a paste with saliva or gum to form the core, which is then decorated with a coloured glass paste mosaic applied with a needle as in enamel-work. The finished bead is fired in a crude oven. This craft, like that of the straw beads mentioned above, is practised by women, and it may well be that the last bead maker of Walata, Lalla Aïcha, is no more.

3
Senegal, the Sahel and Ghana

Burial mounds at Rao in Senegal, thought to be pre-Islamic, perhaps early second millennium AD in date, have produced carnelian, hollow gold and silver beads as necklaces, and also some glass beads. Another Senegalese burial site, at Diakhité sand-pit, near Thiès, is dated to the eighteenth to nineteenth centuries and has numerous beads. Glass, stone, amber, metal and shell beads were found loose or in clay pots along with other ornaments of brass and copper. They obviously derive from the external trade with western Africa that was recorded by early travellers. The burials are attributed to the Serer, a tribal group whose customs involved placing grave goods with the deceased. 13,500 beads were recovered in 1986-8, including beads of amber from the Baltic and of rock crystal; glass trade beads numbered almost twelve thousand, including numerous wound doughnut-shaped beads, faceted glass beads and decorated beads such as chevrons, eye beads and layered drawn beads. Two intact pots seem to have been containers for grave goods, holding metal ornaments as well as beads; the beads seem to date to 1500-1900 approximately, and the earlier ones are presumably heirlooms. In the smaller pot, the beads were strung together, each according to its variety. Many of the beads are datable by analogy with types found in archaeological sites in the eastern United States and the Caribbean.

Excavations at Jenne-Jeno and on the Bandiagara escarpment in Dogon country, both in Mali, have produced beads; Ibn Battuta, who crossed the Sahel in the mid fourteenth century, paid for goods with glass beads as well as salt and spices. Carnelian beads could have come from Cambay in India and glass beads from Egypt and other glass-working areas in the eastern Mediterranean as well as Venice; there is good evidence for a trade network between western Africa and the Mediterranean world both across the Sahara and from Egypt and the Sudan.

Since the better-off people tended to wear fabric clothing, beads might be worn beneath, as in the case of the Senegalese ladies of about 1800 described as wearing ten or twelve strings of glass beads round their hips beneath their clothes, which made a noise when they walked. Demand for beads was enormous; in 1763-4 men and women were described wearing belts of beads 30 cm (1 foot) wide by three or four rows thick.

8. Woman's belt in black, red, blue, yellow and white beads. From Sherbro Island, Sierra Leone, collected before 1875. (Museum of Mankind, London.)

The Bassari live mostly in Guinea, Senegal and Guinea-Bissau, with a few in Gambia. They have preserved a non-Muslim way of life, and their beadwork has been well studied and documented. It includes distinctive *cache-sexes*, 'touraco beak' headband ornaments and bead-decorated baby-carriers. Imported glass beads are recorded among the Bassari from the early twentieth century; before that beads were made of metal or shell. Rules of age-grouping, sex and colour symbolism have governed the way beads were used, and also market availability. Red beads have been used since at least 1907 and perhaps earlier; in the 1930s large dark blue and white beads were available; in the 1940s flat yellow beads became popular, and since about 1955 the only beads for sale have been small green, blue, yellow and black ones. Aluminium became popular after 1930 for beadmaking since it was easy to work; before that iron and copper had been used. Bassari women wear all the beads and ornament that local custom allows, up to several kilograms weight; metal, beads, plaited vegetable fibre and cloth are always combined.

In Sierra Leone, bead ornaments seem to have been worn mostly in association with initiation ceremonies (figure 8); multistring necklets of fine drawn beads seem to be typical, with lengths of grass or fine plastic mixed in to add to the bulk.

Beads of the Sahel and southwards

The Sahel is the territory lying between the Sahara Desert and the savannahs and more fertile lands to the south. It refers mainly to the Upper Niger and Senegal regions where, in a normal year, there is about 125-250 mm (5 to 10 inches) of rain annually. However, this term can be used, as here, to cover the deep hinterland of western Africa, ranging from Mali to the northern parts of Nigeria and Cameroon and as far east as Chad.

The low rainfall over much of this area means that the population tends to consist of nomadic or semi-nomadic settled communities with a low level of subsistence. There is not very much surplus wealth for elaborate bead display. Tuareg jewellery includes hollow silver beads; glass trade beads are worn together with leather-covered Koranic amulets and the *talhakimt*, a glass or agate amulet formed like a ring with a large triangular projection on one side, which derives its form from the 'cross of Agades'. Czechoslovakia is the main source of agate and glass beads for the Muslim market. Large 'amber' beads are often made of copal, glass or plastic.

The Fulani, a semi-nomadic pastoral people of Niger and northern Nigeria, make bracelets of small round beads with a leather inner lining. Before about 1940, they tended to be patterned in black or blue on white; later the range of colours became larger (figure 9). They are often hawked around by Hausa traders.

Over much of this area, Islamic influence means that clothing is of a generally enveloping nature. Bead clothing, as distinct from bead ornaments, comes from parts of north-eastern Nigeria and Cameroon, and also Chad, where traditional practices survived. The bead apron worn by the Sara Madjingai (figure 10) is a type found over much of this area; small cylinder beads in

9. Bead and leather bracelets, Fulani, Niger. Those at the back were collected before 1930, those at the front may be post-1950. (Author's collection.)

10. (Left) Woman's bead and cowrie pubic apron worn at festivals, from the Sara Madjingai, Republic of Central Africa. Bead colours: navy and mid blue, yellow, red whiteheart, white and clear. (Powell-Cotton Museum, Quex Park, Birchington.)

11. (Above) Woman's bead and cowrie pubic apron attributed to the Tiv, northern Nigeria. Bead colours: navy and mid blue, yellow, and red. (Copyright photograph and collection of Marilee Wood.)

12. (Left) Imborivungu ritual 'owl pipe' from the Tiv, northern Nigeria, made of a human femur, with cowrie eyes and small pink beads and *abrus* seeds set in beeswax. (Museum of Mankind, London.)

various colours seem to be characteristic. The triangular pubic apron (figure 11) attributed to the Tiv of northern Nigeria is in a similar tradition; neck and head ornaments made of round glass beads also occur but have been little researched. Among the Kirdi group of tribes in the northern Nigeria and Chad region brass tongue-like 'stirrup' pendants are worn together with round beads, preferably brass ones.

Beads are used to embellish various fertility or ritual figures. Among the Bobo-Fing of Burkina the *batuma* fetish is an anthropomorphic statuette, sometimes the height of a man, covered with cowries, a fertility symbol which safeguards the fields and crops. The Tiv of northern Nigeria had *imborivungu*, an anthropomorphic voice-disguising pipe, usually made of a human femur. These pipes were often embellished with beads (figure 12), red *abrus* seeds or necklaces and had to be 'recharged' periodically by ritual human sacrifice, since they were kept to ensure the fruitfulness of the land. Among the Fali, Adamawa and Dowayo of northern Nigeria and Cameroon, a man will make a doll for his bride to ensure her fecundity; the doll is put in a corner of the house after the first child's birth. Such dolls may be made of a corn-cob and dressed with beads; others are more naturalistic.

Splendid bead 'corsets' and back skirts were worn by Bachama women (figure 13) during the 1920s at the spring festival at Fare, in Adamawa Province. The dance originated in the time when people went out to the bush to cut grass for their chief's horses and held the dance on their return; only local people could take part in the festival.

Beads of Ghana

Ghana, especially in Asante country, was rich in beads, whether hollow gold beads cast by the lost-wax process (figure 3), locally made stone beads (chapter 2) or powder-glass beads (chapter 2), or glass trade beads (figure 14). The wealth generated by exported gold, slaves or ivory enabled the Asante-hene and other Ghanaian rulers to acquire the costly Venetian millefiore in great quantity and variety. Thomas Bowdich, writing in 1819 about his visit to the Asante kingdom, described millefiore beads and powder-glass beads which he called 'aggry' beads. Aggrey (aggry, akori) beads are the subject of an unsolved argument. They have been variously equated with blue glass *segi* beads from Ife or Popo beads from Bénin (formerly Dahomey), blue coral, dichroic blue-green glass, a form of silicate slag, or

13. Bachama women dancing at the spring festival at Fare, northern Nigeria. Note the woman's 'corset' of blue and white beads. Photographed in 1927 by G. M. Clifford. (Copyright: Pitt Rivers Museum, University of Oxford.)

some kind of blue-green stone of the chrysoprase group. The only certainty is that they were highly valued; they may have been blue or blue-green. Bowdich also related how any child that was heir to a kingdom or rich estate was anointed with a prophylactic paste of ground-up aggrey beads, and how these beads were invoked by someone denying a theft. Since beads were often dug from the ground (probably from burial sites or forgotten shrines) there was the belief that by burying them they would breed.

Jean Barbot, an agent of the Royal Company of Africa, wrote an account of the coastal trade of western Africa from Senegal to Angola in 1688 (English translation in 1732); he described the great quantities of Venetian beads worn by the people of the

Gold and Guinea Coasts on their arms, necks and legs and in their hair, the varieties of beads traded and their commercial values. Thomas Phillips in 1694 saw a king (of Ghana) with 'gowns and mantles of rich silver and gold brocaded silks, trimm'd with flowers of small party-colour'd beads, which were pressents made him, as he told us, by white captains, who traded there'.

Archaeological excavations at the former trading station of Elmina in Ghana may go far to enable glass trade beads to be used as a dating indicator, although 'heirloom' beads can be some two or three hundred years older than the rest of the deposit, which might include other closely datable European products. The uses of beads in Ghana include bead necklets on *akua 'ba* fertility dolls, some of minutely small drawn beads hardly more than 1 mm in diameter and 1.5 mm long and so far of unknown origin. Asante goldwork included plated sword hilts and umbrella tops and ornaments cast by the lost-wax process, ranging from large ornaments up to 20 cm (8 inches) across to rings and beads. Gold beads found on the shipwreck site of the *Whydah*, which sank off Cape Cod in 1717, show that designs changed little between then and the late nineteenth century, when numerous gold ornaments were looted at the time of the Ashanti Wars. Such beads were always hollow and often show signs of the fine wax threads used in building up the bead over the clay core, which was removed after casting.

14. String of Venetian glass trade beads, mostly 'lamp' beads, from the Asante, Ghana. (Museum of Mankind, London.)

4
Nigeria

Historical background

Archaeology provides early information on Nigerian beads and beadwork, beginning with the second half of the first millennium BC. An occupation site belonging to the Nok culture has yielded some quartz and tin beads, but the terracottas, with abundant portrayal of multi-stranded bead necklets, armlets and anklets, give evidence of beads worn by both sexes. These beads could have been made of clay, wood and seeds, as well as of stone and metal, and were surely a sign of rank.

Beads of quartz, carnelian, rock crystal and ostrich eggshell have come from Late Stone Age sites in Nigeria (c.600 BC to AD 900); grooved stones may have been used for grinding strung beads to shape.

Later on (c.AD 700 to 1020), at Igbo-Ukwu, in southern Nigeria, one site, Igbo Isaiah, which may have been a shrine, yielded several bronzes, some with beads attached. Many beads were found in rows, as if threaded or sewn on to cloth; a fallen-over pot seems to have contained a great mass of beads. Another site, Igbo Richard, contained a royal burial chamber with a vast quantity of beads, mostly of glass or carnelian. A reconstruction of the burial chamber in the excavation report shows the corpse seated on a stool, wearing regalia including a beaded crown, beaded anklets and armlets made of blue beads threaded in rows on copper wire. Some of the carnelian beads may have been locally made, but most beads must have been imported, perhaps from Venice, the Middle East or India. They probably reached Igbo-Ukwu via overland trade, from North Africa and Egypt, though it is possible that there was a trade route from the Red Sea or the east African coast. The beads and copper found at Igbo-Ukwu may have been given in exchange for ivory and slaves. About 63,000 beads came from Igbo Isaiah, and the two sites yielded over 165,000 beads.

During c.1100-1450, the ancient town of Ife, the spiritual capital of the Yoruba people, produced its famous bronze heads, thought to be made for effigy figures of deceased rulers. Some heads have perforations (two with beads lodged inside) along the hairline, suggesting that an actual veil of beads was attached, rather as present-day Yoruba chiefs wear beaded crowns with long fringes hiding the face. Excavations at Ife have unearthed

15. (Left) The Oni of Ife, southern Nigeria, wearing the *Are* crown during the Olojo festival; the central medallion has four projecting carnelian beads. Photograph taken in 1961. (Copyright: Frank Willett.)

16. (Right) Oba Akenzua II of Benin, photographed in 1959, wearing a crown, multi-strand collar and shirt of coral beads, also ivory plaques round his waist. (Copyright: Frank Willett.)

quartz beads and grinding stones. Numerous glass beads have been found, especially in the Olokun grove, and also crucible fragments with glass traces in blues, greens, dark red and brown, some containing beads. It seems that all local knowledge of glass-working had been forgotten by 1910, when Leo Frobenius found the glassmaking crucibles and beads. Research indicates that from about AD 800 the Ife beadmakers melted down imported beads to make their own. Beads were used in crested crowns, necklets and badges for royalty, face veils, armlets and anklets, though few have survived except as representations on bronzes and terracottas. The *Are* crown worn by the Oni (ruler) of Ife has a frontal crest with four projecting carnelian beads as well as red parrot and white egret feathers (figure 15); this crown is unique in having such a crest, though it is not otherwise like those worn in the bronzes.

The kingdom of Benin, in south-western Nigeria, is the setting for the next stage in the history of beadwork in Nigeria. Traditional history, going back to the late twelfth century, and the records of early travellers and traders provide a background to the beadwork shown on the Benin bronzes and the traditional heavy coral and jasper bead regalia worn by the Oba of Benin (figure 16) on state occasions. Coral, of Mediterranean origin, came to Nigeria and Benin through Portuguese and other traders from the sixteenth century onwards. Red beads, whether of coral, stone (carnelian or bauxite) or glass, were valued in Benin for their 'threatening power', an ability to drive away evil.

At Benin, ownership of the royal beads was the basis of claims to the throne. The annual bead festival, *Ugie Ivie*, is said to have been created by the sixteenth-century Oba Esigie; it recalls the struggle with his brother for a royal coral bead which would be used to proclaim the succession. During the festival all the beads of the Obas, lesser chiefs and royal wives are assembled on the palace altar and the blood of a human sacrifice was poured over them to renew their power. Nowadays a cow's blood is used. The altar is that to Oba Ewuare, the first warrior Oba, who initiated the use of bead regalia during the festival. Coral beads may not be worn until the rites are completed. Coral necklaces were awarded to chiefs and royal officials as a sign of rank; if one was lost or stolen, the necklace-wearer was placed under sentence of death. The royal coral beads are also important for the power (*ase*) that they give to the Oba's words; whatever he says when wearing his beads will surely happen. When wearing his costume the Oba 'is a god'.

Beads and other goods show that western Africa received trade goods from the Mediterranean from at least the early second millennium BC. Trans-Saharan trade may have been going on for considerably longer, since many goods, such as salt, ostrich feathers, wax and slaves, would leave no trace in archaeology.

From about 500 BC to AD 1800 glass beads were almost certainly being made in small workshops in southern India and were probably exported to Africa by Arab merchants and middlemen along with agate and carnelian beads from Cambay. Archaeology indicates that from at least AD 1100 these were traded across the Sahara from east to west. European traders seem to have started by using beads of European manufacture. Before long, imported Indian-manufactured beads and Indian Ocean cowries featured among the trade goods used, perhaps as a result of customer preference.

Jean Barbot, in describing his travels along the West African coast, listed some of his wares and what he got in exchange. Beads are frequently mentioned as trade goods; it is tantalising to read of the many different varieties: 'maccatons, that is, beads of two sorts . . . clouts, galet, martosdes . . . a sort of Bugle called *Pezant* . . . blue and white *margriettas*, red and black large bugles, red and green *galet*, large yellow amber-stones . . . fine crystal beads . . . *Venice* bugles . . . white and black *contecarbe* . . . beads gooseberry-colour, large and small . . . blue long beads' and so on. 'Bugles are very small glass beads, and mostly made at Venice, and sold in strings and clusters.' Barbot also listed the other trade goods he carried, such as bars of iron, cloth or manufactured goods, even second-hand clothes, and what he expected to get in exchange. He also told how 'they break *Venice* coral into four or five parts, which afterwards they mould into any form, on whetstones'.

Yoruba beadwork

The Yoruba occupy most of the south-western quarter of Nigeria and spread over the western border into Bénin (formerly Dahomey). They have an important place in African art because of the quality and the sheer quantity of their output, whether in wood-carving, metalworking or beadwork. Our information about the Yoruba is fuller than for many other peoples, which enables us to understand better the ritual context of bead ornament and bead-working.

Beads here, as elsewhere, are associated with royalty and the priesthood, which are often combined. Yoruba kings, who have

17. A chief's flywhisk from the Yoruba of southern Nigeria or Bénin (Dahomey), made of a cow's tail; bead colours: white, red, yellow, light and royal blue, black. (Museum of Mankind, London.)

18. A chief's footstool covered in leather and beaded with faces of royal ancestors on the sides, and crowns, sceptres and swords on the top, Yoruba, southern Nigeria.   (Copyright: Musée Royal de l'Afrique Centrale, Tervuren, Belgium.)

a variety of titles, are traditionally descended from the sixteen sons of Odudua, the Earth deity; there are, however, far more than that number of kings and lesser chiefs, since a city state could be divided or a new one be founded. Each king has one or more beaded crowns; other beaded regalia may include a robe, boots, slippers, caps, a flywhisk (figure 17), a staff and a footstool (figure 18).

Crowns are the most important element of regalia. The Oni of Ife, the spiritual head of the Yoruba people and successor to Odudua, has by tradition the right to allow or refuse a claim to a crown. Some elements of regalia are vital to ensure this, as demonstrated in the case of the Elepe of Epe. He tried to upgrade his status by claiming the right to wear a beaded crown (figure 19); this was disputed by the other Yoruba chiefs. In 1903 the then Governor of Lagos, Sir William McGregor, invited the Oni of Ife to attend a meeting of the Lagos chiefs and the Native Council, and the Oni disallowed the Elepe's claim. The beaded crown, cap, boots, staff, birds (for attaching to a crown) and other articles were confiscated and soon afterwards presented to the British Museum.

The earliest crowns (said to go back to the eighteenth century) seem to have been fairly simple in design, cap-shaped with a stem on top, and covered with cowrie shells, African-made red jasper or imported coral beads. Later, state crowns became conical, surmounted by one or more birds, with one or more mask faces

19. Beaded crowns from the Yoruba, southern Nigeria. (Left) The crown of the Elepe of Epe, confiscated by the administration, with beaded veil. (Copyright: Museum of Mankind, London.) (Above) Crown modelled on a British state crown, with four royal *okin* birds; bead colours white and clear. (Below) Pillbox-shaped crown beaded in eleven different colours of beads, with two faces of royal ancestors, and detail of one face. This crown, and the one above right, are the sort worn on other than ritual occasions.
(All Museum of Mankind, London.)

on the sides, and with a beaded fringe which screened the king's face. The faces are said to allude to the king's all-seeing ability; the birds represent *okin*, the royal bird. When the king's own face is hidden by a bead fringe, he is no longer a man but a god, and it is death to look on his face; for similar reasons his feet must not touch the ground, and so he wears beaded footwear and uses a beaded footstool. A chief was supposed to avoid looking inside his crown as there were powerful magical forces within.

Crowns and other elaborate beadwork were made by specialists such as the Adeshina family of Efon-Alaiye. A bead-worker works in private, in his home or a room in the chief's palace. Women are not allowed to do this work, as they might pass the secrets outside the family. In making a crown, a conical basketry framework is made and covered with starched cotton cloth as a foundation for the small seed beads, which are strung on cotton thread and tacked to the surface of the crown in the planned design. Sometimes the pattern is traced on to the foundation; sometimes the beader works from memory or dream inspiration. A relief face might be moulded with shaped pieces of cloth dipped in starch; figures of birds in the round are made similarly with nails, porcupine or bird quills for beaks, some with separately formed wings and actual white feathers. These birds may be sewn on or attached by a peg. Some motifs derive from Islam, such as pendent triangular flaps (charm cases) and the interlace ('Hausa') knot. The inside of a crown was lined with cloth which hides the stitches, and the style of print can sometimes give the age of the crown. An elaborate crown might take six months to make.

One ruler, the Olokuku of Okuku, owns twelve major crowns, 21 crowns based on the shape of the British crown, eleven beaded caps of various shapes, four beaded lawyer's wigs and four other lesser crowns. The Olokuku wears different crowns or caps according to the occasion or ritual of the moment. The crowns play an important part in the annual Oloku festival, which lasts for seven days. On the fifth day the entire treasure is spread out on elaborate appliqué cloths in the palace before being blessed by the Olokuku's mother; on the final day the Olokuku wears each of the twelve crowns in sequence, to the accompaniment of its particular song.

The Yoruba use beads with free inventiveness; the strung beads are full of vibrant life and without formal constraint, especially in a spiritual context, such as the design on an Ifa diviner's bag or an *ibeji* coat (see below). Glass beads were

20. Fan from the Yoruba, southern Nigeria, with velveteen backing, beaded on the front with the face in slight relief. Bead colours: black, white, Indian red, two yellows, green and royal blue. (Museum of Mankind, London.)

probably not available before the mid seventeenth century and may not have been used in quantity for a further hundred years; old glass beads tend to be somewhat larger (about 3-4 mm in diameter) than recent ones. Opaque, clear and metallic glass beads are used in blocks or in medley, sometimes using twenty or more different bead types and colours in one piece, with small and long faceted beads and larger seed beads to vary the surface; areas are outlined in contrast colour, and the surface shimmers in the light. Recently plastic beads have been used; because of their non-reflectivity, the effect is inferior.

Beadwork is not only used on royal crowns and regalia; it plays an important part in enhancing religious apparatus such as diviners' vestments and bags for the Ifa cult, dance panels, sheaths for ritual staffs, fans (figure 20) and clothing for figures of deceased twins (*ibeji*). *Ibeji* are wooden figures about 25 cm (10 inches) high, carved to represent one or both of twins who have died in infancy. The Yoruba have an exceptional incidence of twin births (45 per 1000), with perhaps half of those the

21. 'Royal jar' with one ancestor face on the side, and two *okin* birds on the lid, from Efon-Alaiye, Yorubaland, southern Nigeria. Beaded in fourteen different colours and sorts of bead. (Museum of Mankind, London.)

hereditary fraternal twin births. The mother, and later any surviving twin, look after this figure, feed it, anoint it and dress it in beads. If the *ibeji* comes from a chiefly family the beads will not be just a string round the neck or waist, but a densely beaded all-enveloping coat. Since twins are associated with Shango, the god of thunder, zigzag patterns in red and white are common. Certain colours 'belong' to certain spirits, such as yellow and green beads with Ifa divination.

While crowns and regalia, diviners' bags and priestly vestments are among the better known examples of Yoruba beadwork, there is a beaded mask made in the style of a conical fringed crown at the Leeds City Museum, a free-standing group of figures 109 cm (42 inches) high in the Museum of Mankind which may be a dance head-dress, and a variety of containers including bottles, boxes (figure 21) and covered bowls on stands.

5
The Bight of Biafra to Gabon

This heading comprises south-eastern Nigeria from the Niger delta eastward to southern Gabon and includes the Cameroon Grasslands, a major beadwork-producing area. Some very interesting beadwork also comes from the Kalabari, Ibo and Ibibio of Nigeria, the island of Fernando Po and the Fang of Gabon.

The Kalabari use important-looking beads, particularly coral, which feature in the costume that women wear during the *Iria Bo* rituals. These cover the period from puberty to the birth of the first child, and the sequence of ceremonies is accompanied by different sets of glass and coral bead ornament and clothing which follow strict rules and are also a means of displaying family wealth. Pillbox hats encrusted with coral beads, several massive coral beads on necklets, necklaces and arm ornaments, heart-shaped pendants covered with coral beads and coral-beaded staffs are among the regalia of a fully graduated *Iria Bo*, together with the best clothing that she is entitled to wear.

European contact with western Africa goes back to the late fifteenth century. In addition to supplying European traders with ivory, gold, slaves and palm oil, African craftsmen made 'curiosities' (which we might call souvenirs) for sale. Afro-Portuguese ivory carvings, made in Sierra Leone and Loango, form the best known group of early craftwork made for export. Such souvenirs were also made in beadwork; in some cases the craft may have been taught in mission schools. Village headmen or title-holders in secret societies among the Ibo wear beaded caps, similar to European smoking caps. Perhaps they were copies of those worn by off-duty German army officers before 1918, when Cameroon was a German colony and sphere of influence. Beaded smoking caps were popular in the mid to late nineteenth century, whether made by European ladies for their menfolk, or copied and made for sale as souvenirs by the American Indians of eastern Canada. The cap shown in figure 22, with the German eagle, described as from Cameroon, could be of European make or an African-made copy for the use of some important man of German Cameroon. The bag (figure 23), collected by Sir Harry Johnston, is an unusual example of traditional Ibibio design, with its flowing vegetable-derived motifs, adapted to applied beadwork decoration; this may well

22. (Above) Black velvet cap beaded with flowers and the German eagle, and with a beaded plait from the crown. Probably Ibo, from south-eastern Nigeria or south-western Cameroon. (Museum of Mankind, London.)

23. (Right) Bag from the Ibibio of south-eastern Nigeria, collected before 1890 by Sir Harry Johnston. Black and turquoise-blue barrel-shaped beads; the reverse side has black, white, red and yellow beads of similar type. (Museum of Mankind, London.)

have been made for European use.

The Bubi of Fernando Po, an island in the corner of the Bight of Biafra, have a distinctive form of beadwork. Superficially, the beads look like ostrich eggshell, but they are made from the shells of a conch, *Strombus bubonius*, in a similar technique, except that the edges of the shell discs are not ground smooth but are left chipped, albeit carefully. The most typical ornaments are made of plaited strings or bands of these beads (figure 24), which were worn by both sexes, though women usually had more than men, who wore only garters or armbands, unless they were headmen. Strings of shell beads also served as currency.

Cameroon Grasslands

The Grasslands form the central part of the interior of Cameroon. As the name suggests, it is an upland savannah region of rolling grassland interspersed with woodland. Cameroon was a German colony, which was divided between Britain and France after the First World War, with the Grasslands area going to France. As a consequence of this history, German museums own most of the early and fine beaded objects that are not still in Cameroon, where the great majority remain in royal treasure-houses.

The Bamileke people, including the Bamenda, are the largest tribal group in the Grasslands; others are the Bamoun (or Bamum) and the Bafut. They are Bantu speakers and have many cultural features in common. There were formerly a great many chiefdoms, each under their own chief (*fon*, *mfon*); belief in a Great God and ancestor worship played an important part in their religion, though the Bamoun converted to Islam after 1896.

Beads used in Grasslands beadwork fall into two main groups. One is that of the long cylinder beads which are usually dark blue, dull terracotta red (perhaps in imitation of coral) or white. These are about 5 mm (¼ inch) in diameter and 10-15 mm (½ inch) long and are often used in covering royal ancestor figures. They were probably made in Bohemia in the nineteenth century and imported by Hausa and Fulani traders. They are rated old and valuable, and their use on a carving is a sign that the piece is likely to be old (before 1914). However, the beadwork cover to a carving may be repaired or replaced, and old beads reused, so the rule is not infallible. Chevron beads (figure 25), some as large as 7 cm (nearly 3 inches), appear on neck ornaments worn by chiefs and other people of rank, and they, like the old cylinder beads, are highly valued. The other group includes the round

24. Belt and two armlets made of plaited strands of disc beads made of conch shells, from Fernando Po. (Museum of Mankind, London.)

25. Glass beads from Cameroon; the two upper rows are worn by women as waist belts; the chevron beads, especially the large one, were reserved for chiefs or court officials. (Museum of Mankind, London.)

(seed) beads found throughout western Africa, or smaller cylinder beads (about 5 mm, ¼ inch) long. These also are used in beadwork covers and are relatively recent, from the early twentieth century onward.

The preferred bead colours are black, shades of blue, white, red and pink; green, yellow and orange occur on the more recent pieces. Black (or dark blue) is the colour of night, and the bond between the ancestral dead and the living; white, the colour of bones and death, also stands for purity, while red is the colour of blood and life. Cowries from East Africa and the Indian Ocean were used as a sign of wealth and prestige, especially on thrones and stools. Designs are stylised and geometrical, often symbolic. The commonest show the leopard (emblem of royalty), the snake (symbolising royal power and the ability to attack on two fronts), the frog (symbolising fertility and cleverness) and the spider (representing a link with the ancestors, and wisdom).

Above all, the beadwork of the Cameroon Grasslands is used to cover wood-carvings and other articles. The right to use such beaded objects was reserved to the king or chief, his close family and important retainers. Wood-carvers might come from within a royal lineage or one serving the royal family; Fon Yu, ruler of Kom (*c.*1865-1912), is reputed to have carved one of the near-lifesize throne figures which were central to the installation ceremonies of a new *fon*. A carving might be worked in some detail even before covering with beads (figure 27). The beading

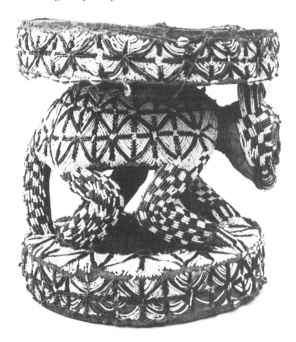

26. Chief's leopard stool, probably Bamileke, Cameroon Grasslands, Cameroon. The motifs on the body are stylised spiders; the bead colours are royal blue, white, yellow and red. (Museum of Mankind, London.)

27. Detail of figure 26. Carved cowries can be seen under the beading of the basal rim; where beads have broken away the sewing method is visible. (Museum of Mankind, London.)

technique can be seen in the same illustration: the stool with leopard support (figure 26) is covered with coarse raphia cloth or burlap, sometimes anchored with small pegs or twine; the beads are threaded on fibre or raphia thread and sewn in 'lazy stitch' every five beads or so, depending on size. The beading is often directional, following the design or the contours of the carving, and long and round beads are mixed to enhance the effect. In the old days bead-workers were specialist professionals who worked with beads supplied by the king, who also encouraged his wives and daughters to make small beaded objects.

Since the use of beads, which came into the country through external trade (a royal monopoly), was under the king's control, it followed that regalia to strengthen the king's power would be decorated with beads and kept in the royal treasure-house. That of the Fon of Bamoun is now a museum as well as a source of insignia to be used as the occasion demands. The *catalogue raisonné* of this collection (Geary, 1983) gives an excellent idea of the scope of a royal treasure, its background and how it accumulated. German collectors in the colonial domination period between 1902 and 1914 managed to collect a number of important pieces including a royal throne with two ancestor figures and footrest closely similar to that in Foumban; this was a diplomatic gift from King Njoya to the Kaiser, and it seems that the Museum für Völkerkunde in Berlin has the original.

It was the custom to have the Fon's effigy carved during his reign together with those of his titled royal women; such figures are present at the funeral ceremonies of a deceased Fon and at his successor's enstoolment, thereby ensuring the presence of the ancestors and continuity of rule. Such effigies might be free-standing or appear as the backrest of a royal stool; there is a great variety in size, posture and manner of covering, usually bead-work, but sometimes entirely in cowries. Other figures were the 'cup-bearers', which hold a cup to receive offerings in funeral ceremonies. Beaded calabashes (figure 28) are perhaps the commonest, also the most instantly recognisable and well known examples of Grasslands beadwork. Their original function was to hold skulls or skull fragments from the royal cemetery, and they were placed on small stool-like stands, themselves often beaded and carved. They are generally empty nowadays and are simply royal display objects. Such calabashes have been described as containers for palm wine which was poured out in rituals for the king; since the long neck is often in more than one piece and is sewn on to the body, they are not water-tight and this

28. Two beaded calabashes, one with the stopper shaped like an elephant, the other like a chameleon. Bead colours are white, navy and royal blue, and red. Cameroon Grasslands, Cameroon. (Museum of Mankind, London.)

29. (Below) Head-dress mask surmounted by two leopards beaded in black, white, orange and turquoise blue; the tails are covered in red cloth. Cameroon Grasslands, Cameroon. (Museum of Mankind, London.)

30. (Above) Two elephant masks, Cameroon Grasslands, Cameroon. (Left) Bead colours are white, orange, pink, two greens and two blues on an indigo cloth backing. Height 137 cm (54 inches). (Right) Beaded with cowrie shells on a brown cloth ground. Height 136 cm (53½ inches). (Museum of Mankind, London.)

identification must be discounted. A king may have up to a dozen calabashes on show, together with beaded ancestor figures, stools, trophy skulls, swords with beaded hilts and sheaths, flywhisks with beaded handles and tobacco pipes with long beaded stems. His costume might include such beaded objects as a mitre-like crown, a tunic, an imitation beard and various ornaments, including a necklet of large chevron beads. The royal women wore their own style of bead necklets and girdles, normally of small round beads.

Masks, used in secret societies and associated with the royal court, were sometimes beaded. Wooden buffalo face masks, covered with long cane beads, fall within the sculptural tradition of the Grasslands. Summit or head-dress masks, on a basketry and cloth foundation and beaded, consist of a cap surmounted by a stylised leopard with a long tail; or they could be made of wood (figure 29). Beaded masks were usually made on a basketry and cloth foundation; the elephant masks of warrior secret societies found among the various Bamileke tribes are the best known. Early examples in Germany were collected in 1903-11, while some are made for the tourist market today. A typical elephant mask (figure 30) is made with a cap-like head covering, itself covered with indigo blue cloth, with two large circular ear-flaps and a long oblong flap in front of and behind the masker. Face, ears and 'trunks' are beaded in geometric designs in lazy stitch; the trunks are backed with burlap, sometimes with a cane stiffener at the very bottom. The maskers wear long body-hiding tunics and often a tall hat with a flaring crown (figure 31) of basketwork covered with beads on a cloth base. The true effect of such masks lies in the swirling movement of the beaded flaps as the maskers gyrate in the dance.

Small figures, under 46 cm (18 inches) high, covered with beads

31. (Left) Hat worn by elephant maskers. Basketry with cloth covering. Bead colours: white, pink, yellow, green and two blues. Cameroon Grasslands, Cameroon. (Museum of Mankind, London.)

32. (Right) Skullcap with fringe of twisted fibre, beaded in white, red and blue on a palm-rib base. From the Fang, Gabon. (Museum of Mankind, London.)

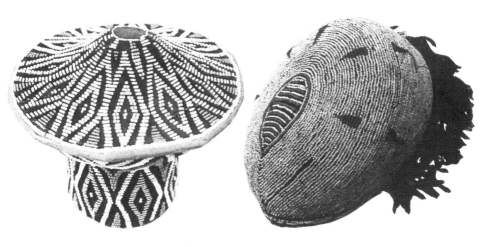

33. Helmet-shaped head-dress ornamented with cowrie shells and white buttons, with a fringe of royal blue and red beads. From the Fang, Gabon. (Leeds City Museum.)

and coix seeds (Job's tears) are made for sale to Europeans and are not truly traditional except in technique.

The Fang (or Pangwe, Pahouin) of southern Cameroon, Equatorial Guinea and Gabon had beaded head-dresses, some like caps (figure 32), some in varied helmet shapes. These have been described by G. Tessmann and the Duke of Mecklenburg, who visited the area at about the same time, both publishing in 1913. These head-dresses were made by braiding the hair with raphia, bast and palm strips as a foundation for the decoration. The process of making such a coiffure might take weeks rather than days, and the wearer needed a special headrest at night to keep the arrangement intact. Wigs, worn on a shaven scalp, tended to replace them; they were made in much the same way, and some examples are in European museums. They are recognisable by the foundation of palm-rib slivers whipped together with raphia, and the tendency to have a frontal fringe made of small loops of beads or elongated whipped knots of fibre cord. The beads are usually in the primary colours of red, blue and white, sometimes with yellow and clear colourless beads. The helmet-style head-dresses (figure 33) may have a line of brass studs, several rows of white china buttons or sometimes cowries. Probably among the Fang, as elsewhere, white buttons were a cheap substitute for the costly cowries of the Indian Ocean. Some of these head-dresses and coiffures had long streamers, whether of bead strings or plaited hair; Tessmann recorded several types occurring in different areas although the finest were in the south.

Both men and women wore them, only taking them off if in mourning or on a raid. It is tempting to see them as inspired by sixteenth-century helmets, but they are an elaboration of actual coiffures such as are shown on Fang figure carvings. Mecklenburg illustrates many elaborate hairstyles seen on his expedition, often enhanced with arrangements of beads. Such head-dresses, although current in the earliest years of the twentieth century, died out soon after.

Beaded belts (figure 34) were made in Gabon and the Republic of Congo by the M'Pongwe and related tribes; in both countries wild rubber was an export crop, which doubtless went to pay for the imported beads and buttons.

34. (Below and bottom) Beaded belts from the M'Pongwe of the Congo Republic and Gabon in a variety of bead colours. (Museum of Mankind, London.)

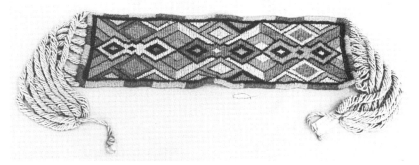

35. King Bope Mabiinc of the Kuba, Zaire, in the full *bwaantshy* state costume. Photographed before 1955. (Copyright: Musée Royal de l'Afrique Centrale, Tervuren, Belgium.)

6
Zaire and Angola

Zaire

Each of the areas of West and Central Africa has its own typical beads and Zaire is no exception. Beads are often strung on a thickish raphia cord and, perhaps on account of this, they tend to be rather large, with big perforations. Large round or ovoid beads, white, opalescent and blue; annular beads, mostly blue; short drawn canes and faceted beads, usually in shades of blue, may come strung on raphia in bunches for currency. Such beads may be on a long multiple string as a woman's waistband. White with turquoise, mid blue and royal or navy blue seems to be a favourite colour combination; black, red and yellow are more recently popular. Round ('seed') beads are less prevalent here than in other parts of Africa.

Cowrie shells also feature in Zairean beadwork, both because of the white colour and as an indicator of wealth, since they are expensive imports from the Indian Ocean. Unlike the other areas already discussed, Zaire had direct contacts with East Africa through Arab slavers and traders speaking Swahili or its related *lingua franca*, Lingala. Sometimes white porcelain buttons were used as a substitute for cowries.

The best known Zairean beadwork is that associated with the royal court of the Kuba, a tribal group living in the Kasai region of central Zaire. Their oral history records go back to at least the sixteenth century, and they became powerful under the Bushoong in the seventeenth and eighteenth centuries. The hierarchy of the old-established court is the setting for a variety of costumes in which the wearer is entitled to certain ornaments according to his rank and office. Cowries are used extensively on clothing and luxury objects, since they are both currency and decoration. They are attached in various ways: slit uppermost, dome uppermost, or secured by one end to stand upwards. Only the king is allowed to wear cowries in bulk. Beads are used lavishly and rank ahead of cowries in court decoration, although feathers are a more important indication of status.

The *bwaantshy* costume (figure 35) (the only one reserved exclusively for the reigning king), which belongs to the present king Kot a-Mbweeki III, weighs 84 kg (rather more than 13 stone) when complete. It is no wonder that it is worn only on the most important ceremonial occasions. The court tailor makes a

36. Waist pendant on strap, ornamented with cowries, and beaded in blue and white on raphia cloth. Kuba, Zaire. (Museum of Mankind, London.)

new *bwaantshy* costume for each king on his accession, since that of the old king is buried with him, after being worn for one day only by the regent to establish the continuing authority of the monarchy. Nearly fifty elements go to the making of this costume, which includes an elaborate tunic, similar openwork leggings, broad necklets, long ceremonial girdles with twenty to thirty pendent ornaments, shoulder circlets secured by embroidered hands, an elaborate head-dress in the shape of a small house with many feathers on top, a rich browband with a conusshell disc, an artificial beard made of beads and cowries, numerous armlets and anklets of both beadwork and brass,

37. (Left) Rear view of a Kuba crown, beaded in white, pale and royal blue in the *imboolo* interlace pattern. (Museum of Mankind, London.)

38. (Right) Chief's crown from the Leele, a subgroup of the Kuba, beaded in *imboolo* interlace pattern in red, yellow and royal blue beads, and bordered with cowries. Collected in the late 1940s. (Museum of Mankind, London.)

gloves and shoes. During the long process of dressing, the king's wives sing propitiatory songs to soothe him. Designs on girdles (figure 36) and headgear (figures 37, 38) reflect the Kuba love of intricate interlace derived from plaited basketry; each pattern is named, and many are allusive or symbolic.

This costume is perhaps the most extreme example of conspicuous status-enhancing display found in Africa. Joseph Cornet has listed nine main sorts of ceremonial costume worn by the king and other members of the royal family; he also describes the great variety of costume and number of body ornaments used, usually embellished with beads and cowries. Most of these may be worn only by nobles or officials of a certain rank; infringement attracts a severe penalty.

'Baskets of wisdom', a symbol rather than a container, also heavily beaded in the Kuba interlacing style, are carried by important officials at court. Royal drums, carved of wood and covered with cowries and beads on a raphia cloth base, were devised by King Kot Mabiintsh ma-Kyeen in the 1920s.

Little was known of the Kuba before the early years of the twentieth century, and it seems that the elaboration of dress and ornament described above is partly a consequence of the mass importation of cowries and beads. Earlier royal display seems to have consisted of voluminous embroidered raphia clothing, ivory and brass armlets, heirloom beads and leopard skins. Exquisitely and intricately carved seats, drinking horns and cups, pipes and sword handles showed that the king had the finest craftsmen to serve him.

Other parts of the Zaire region have crowns in the form of beaded head-dresses. For instance, Pende chiefs have a crown with two lateral horns; the Yaka have a rather similar one. Both are made on a basketry foundation covered with short cane beads, usually with a design in chevrons or triangles. Early travellers and missionaries have left sketches or descriptions of the crowns and other ornaments worn by African royalty such as Mwata Kazembe of the Lunda in eastern Zaire. 'Heirloom beads', often eye or chevron beads, worn on their own or together with leopard or human teeth, may form a chief's necklet.

39. Small sword, the hilt beaded in a design of lozenges and triangles. Small beads, the colours in two blues, two yellows, pink and white, sewn brickwise. Length 71 cm (28 inches). Probably from Zaire. (Museum of Mankind, London.)

40. (Right) Burial mask from the Kuba, Zaire, the face surrounded with cowries and white, black and blue cylinder beads, the nose and eyes made with white, green and blue beads. (National Museums of Scotland, Edinburgh.)

41. (Left) Mask for the Mbudye society, Tabwa, eastern Zaire. Monkey fur with white, yellow, orange, red and black beads. (Copyright: The Stanley Collection, University of Iowa Museum of Art, Iowa City, Iowa, USA.)

Beads serve as status markers. A sword with a beaded hilt (figure 39) probably belonged to a chief; his staff or headrest might be enhanced with beads; a figure carving might have some beads, either to show its importance or as a thank-offering to the ancestor represented.

Sometimes masks were embellished with beads; again the Kuba provide the best known examples, which are associated with court masquerades and belong to the Kuba idiom of a basketry foundation covered with raphia cloth embroidered with beads and cowries in an interlace design. The *mwaashambooy* mask, topped by a stylised elephant's trunk, is well known and a favourite subject for 'airport art'; other masks are made to be worn at funerals (figure 40). Cornet (1982) illustrates how, using templates, such masks were made up of separate beaded elements; Kuba crowns were put together in much the same way. The Tabwa of eastern Zaire have masks made of beads applied in lazy stitch on a fabric base (figure 41), which may be associated with the Mbudye secret society. The central spiral on the browband represents the 'eye' of an earth spirit; the triangles are 'doors' for other spirits. This design and the bead colours, yellow and orange as well as the more usual white, red and black, are similar to those of the head-dresses worn by diviners of the Bulumbu possession cult among the Tabwa and neighbouring

42. (Left) Head-dress of *nganga* (diviner) of the Luba, Zaire. Red, white and blue beads with cowries. (Copyright: Musée Royal de l'Afrique Centrale, Tervuren, Belgium.)

43. (Right) Skullcap head-dress from the Ngbaka, northern Zaire, beaded in white, mid and dark blue beads on a palm-rib base. (Copyright: Musée Royal de l'Afrique Centrale, Tervuren, Belgium.)

peoples. Luba diviners (figure 42) have rather similar head-dresses.

The Luba have a curious beaded object called *lukasa*, a rectangular board often with a human head on top, and having beads fixed in an apparently random pattern on the flat surface. It serves as a coded mnemonic for initiates of the Mbudye society.

Ordinary people also used bead ornament. Old photographs show Sango men and women of northern Zaire with bonnet-like beaded coiffures; the Ngbaka, also of northern Zaire, had basketwork skullcaps (figure 43) beaded in white and shades of blue. Throughout Zaire, both sexes might wear strings of beads round the neck, or bandolier-wise, or as armlets or anklets. Some can only be identified as Zairean by the raphia threading or the subtle reddish-brown tint given by camwood (the red wood powder is mixed with castor oil and used as a body cosmetic). Traditional women's clothing included one or more strings of beads round the hips which might include an amulet to ensure fertility and easy childbirth. Older country women still wear such beads under their European-style clothing. The Yaka, and the adjacent Holo and Suku, make beaded panels in black, white, red, yellow, green and blue, made from round ('seed') beads sewn brickwise with cotton thread and fringed. They are about 26-30 cm (10-12 inches) wide, patterned in triangles, chevrons and diagonal bands, and look like pubic aprons. They are, however, breast covers and seem to be a fairly recent result

44. Belt, beaded in dark and turquoise blue, white and red, from the Chokwe of Zaire. (Copyright: Musée Royal de l'Afrique Centrale, Tervuren, Belgium.)

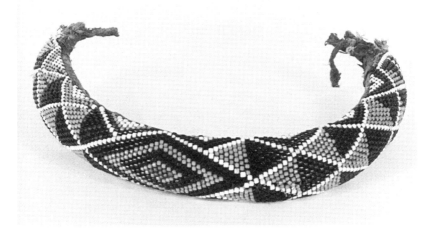

(perhaps since the 1930s) of the greater availability of beads and changing dress fashion.

Ivory pendants in Zaire almost rank as beads. Small replica masks were worn among the Pende; the Luba and Hungaan made female torsos, often of hippopotamus or wart-hog ivory, which preserve the curve of the tusk. The Songye made stick-like pendants, some ending in a human head, ornamented with ring-and-dot marks.

Angola

The beadwork of northern Angola is in much the same tradition as that of Zaire; the Chokwe span the borders of both countries and even spill over into western Zambia. A chief's head-dress attributed to the 'Lunda-Chokwe', and rather similar to those of the Pende and Yaka, is patterned with blue and white concentric circles and rectangles in round beads on a basketwork foundation. A Chokwe chief's ceremonial axe handle may be wound round with small round beads. Women's headbands worn in Huila province are beaded in red, white and blue lozenges and triangles with brow fringes and long side strings. The Chokwe waist ornament, patterned in mid and dark blue, white and red lozenges and triangles (figure 44), has beads similar to those used by the Pende and Yaka in their chiefs' crowns.

The beadwork of southern Angola has already been touched upon in *Beads and Beadwork of East and South Africa,* since the Ovambo straddle the border between Angola and Namibia, and the Kwanyama of southern Angola have many cultural similarities. Women's ochre-stained leather clothing and unmarried girls' 'corsets' of many strands of ostrich-eggshell beads are worn on both sides of the border. Kwanyama women's prestige ornaments also include leather pendant straps ornamented with conus-shell discs or roundish domed beads with incised decoration made of elephant ivory or wart-hog tusk; these also occur in Namibia. Other locally made beads are made of iron or copper, strung on thongs into heavy anklets or necklets. The Ovambo (or Ambo) have fertility dolls, cylindrical or dumb-bell shaped, ornamented with beads wound spirally over their bodies; those of the Kwanyama are more naturalistic. Often these beads are small drawn canes about 2 mm in diameter; it is tempting to think that they originate in Portugal or Spain as they are unlike those found in other parts of Africa. A long string of these small beads is used to make multi-strand hip belts, worn by Kwanyama married women. They also wear massive beaded roll collars,

45. Kwanyama woman with large conus-shell pendant, massive beaded collar, and beaded coiffure, photographed in 1937 by Neverovski for the Misses Powell-Cotton.

made of a coiled twig or cord foundation which may include a coiled string of beads as part of the structure, which is held together by bast ties or is densely covered by beads coiled diagonally over most of the surface (figure 45). The beads are often ground down flat on one surface and appear old; they are treated as heirlooms and handed down from mother to daughter. As recently as the 1950s, coiffures were created in elaborate shapes (figure 45) using ochred mud to form structures in which the woman's own beads were set in patterns; as the hair grew, the coiffure would be re-set. Women of rank or seniority would have the greatest number of beads, including imported heirlooms, often Venetian 'eye' beads.

7
Museums

Many museums with an ethnographical collection will have some beads and beadwork from West and Central Africa. The principal ones are listed below. Intending visitors are advised to find out the opening times before making a special journey.

Great Britain

Birmingham Museum and Art Gallery, Chamberlain Square, Birmingham, West Midlands B3 3DH. Telephone: 021-235 2834.

Brighton Art Gallery and Museum, Church Street, Brighton, East Sussex BN1 1UE. Telephone: 0273 603005.

Cambridge University Museum of Archaeology and Anthropology, Downing Street, Cambridge CB2 3DZ. Telephone: 0223 333516 or 337733.

Glasgow Art Gallery and Museum, Kelvingrove, Glasgow G3 8AG. Telephone: 041-357 3929.

Horniman Museum and Library, London Road, Forest Hill, London SE23 3PQ. Telephone: 081-699 1872, 2339 or 4911.

Leeds City Museum, Calverley Street, Leeds, West Yorkshire LS1 3AA. Telephone: 0532 462632.

Liverpool Museum, William Brown Street, Liverpool, Merseyside L3 8EN. Telephone: 051-207 0001.

The Manchester Museum, The University of Manchester, Oxford Road, Manchester M13 9PL. Telephone: 061-275 2634.

Marischal Museum, Marischal College, Aberdeen AB9 1AS. Telephone: 0224 273132.

Museum of Mankind (Ethnography Department of the British Museum), 6 Burlington Gardens, London W1X 2EX. Telephone: 071-323 8043.

Pitt Rivers Museum, Parks Road, Oxford OX1 3PP. Telephone: 0865 270927.

Powell-Cotton Museum, Quex Park, Birchington, Kent CT7 0BH. Telephone: 0843 42168.

Royal Museum of Scotland, Chambers Street, Edinburgh EH1 1JF. Telephone: 031-225 7534.

Belgium

Musée Royal de l'Afrique Centrale, Steenweg op Leuven 15, 1980 Tervuren.

France
Musée de l'Homme, Palais de Chaillot, Place du Trocadéro, 75016 Paris.

Germany
Linden-Museum Stuttgart, Staatliches Museum für Völkerkunde, Hegelplatz 1, 7000 Stuttgart, Baden-Württemberg.
Museum für Völkerkunde, Arnimallee 23-27, 1000 Berlin 33.

Netherlands
Afrika Museum, Berg en Dal, 8071 GU Nijmegen, Gelderland.
Tropenmuseum (Koninklijk Instituut voor den Tropen), Linnaeusstraat 2, 1092 AD Amsterdam.

8
Further reading

Most of the information is scattered among articles in periodicals, which can best be found in libraries.

Beier, Ulli. *Yoruba Beaded Crowns*. Ethnographica, London, 1982.
Brincard, Marie-Thérèse. *Beauty by Design*. African-American Institute, New York, 1984.
Cornet, Joseph. *Art royal Kuba*. Sipiel, Milan, 1982.
Delarozière, Marie-Françoise. *Les Perles de Mauritanie*. Édisud, Aix-en-Provence, 1985.
Dubin, Lois. *The History of Beads*. Thames and Hudson, 1987.
Fagg, William. *Yoruba Beadwork*. Lund Humphries, 1980.
Fisher, Angela. *Africa Adorned*. Collins, 1984.
Francis, Peter. *The Glass Trade Beads of Europe*. Center for Bead Research, Lake Placid, New York, 1988.
Gabus, Jean. *Au Sahara*, volume III. Editions de la Baconnière, Neuchâtel, 1982.
Geary, Christraud. *Things of the Palace*. Steiner Verlag, Wiesbaden, 1983.
Harter, Pierre. *Arts anciens du Cameroun*. Arts d'Afrique Noire, Arnouville, 1986.
Hodge, Alison. *Nigeria's Traditional Crafts*. Ethnographica, London, 1982.

Northern, Tamara. *Royal Art of Cameroon.* Hopkins Center Art Galleries, Dartmouth College, Hanover, New Hampshire, 1973.

Northern, Tamara. *The Sign of the Leopard.* William Benton Museum of Art, University of Connecticut, Storrs, Connecticut, 1975.

Ryder, A. F. C. *Benin and the Europeans, 1486-1897.* Longman, 1969.

Van der Zwan, Nelleke. *Oog voor Kralen.* Afrika Museum, Berg en Dal, 1985.

Useful articles and monographs by Peter Francis, Christraud Geary, Alastair Lamb, Thurstan Shaw and others can be found in *African Arts* (UCLA); *African Studies; Nigeria* magazine; *Ornament* (formerly *Bead Journal*); publications of the Center for Bead Research, Lake Placid, New York; Institut Français d'Afrique Noire (IFAN); Royal Anthropological Institute, London; Musée Royal de l'Afrique Centrale, Tervuren, Belgium; Society of Bead Researchers, Ottawa, Canada.

Index

Page numbers in italic refer to illustrations.